HEMINGWAY'S
SPAIN

BY BARNABY CONRAD
PHOTOGRAPHS BY LOOMIS DEAN

CHRONICLE BOOKS · SAN FRANCISCO

HEMINGWAY'S SPAIN

Grateful acknowledgément is made for the permission to reprint:

James Morris, quoted from *Presence of Spain*. Reprinted by permission of Julian Bach Literary Agency, Inc. Copyright 1963 James Morris.

V. S. Pritchett, quoted from *A Man of Letters: Selected Essays*. Copyright 1985 by V. S. Pritchett. Reprinted by permission of Random House Inc.

Ernest Hemingway, excerpted from *The Dangerous Summer*. Copyright 1960 Ernest Hemingway. Copyright 1985 Mary Hemingway, John Hemingway, Patrick Hemingway, and Gregory Hemingway. Reprinted with the permission of Charles Scribner's Sons, an imprint of Macmillan Publishing Company.

Ernest Hemingway, excerpted from *By-Line: Ernest Hemingway*, edited by William White. Copyright 1967 Mary Hemingway. Reprinted with the permission of Charles Scribner's Sons, an imprint of Macmillan Publishing Company.

Ernest Hemingway, excerpted from *Ernest Hemingway Selected Letters 1917–1961* edited by Carlos Baker. Copyright 1981 Carlos Baker and The Ernest Hemingway Foundation, Inc. Reprinted with the permission of Charles Scribner's Sons, an imprint of Macmillan Publishing Company.

Julian Gray, reprinted with the permission of Julian Gray.

Carlos Baker, excerpted from *Ernest Hemingway, A Life Story*. Copyright 1969 Carlos Baker. Reprinted with the permission of Charles Scribner's Sons.

Allen Josephs, quoted from the "Hemingway Review." Reprinted with the permission of Allen Josephs.

The author would also like to thank Maurice Neville for unlimited access to his Hemingwayana and John Hadley Nicanor Hemingway for his encouragement in the project.

Printed in Japan

Library of Congress Cataloging in Publication Data

Conrad, Barnaby, 1922–
    Hemingway's Spain / Barnaby Conrad : photographs by Loomis
Dean
        p.   cm.
    ISBN 0-87701-561-9. – ISBN 0-87701-547-3 (pbk.)
    1. Hemingway, Ernest, 1899–1966 – knowledge – Spain – Pictorial
works.   2. Spain – Description and travel – 1981- –Views.
3. Literary landmarks – Spain – Pictorial works.   4. Spain in
literature – Pictorial works.   5. Bullfiights – Spain – Pictorial works.
I. Dean, Loomis.   II. Title.
PS3515.E37Z58463   1989
813'.52 – dc19   89-31215
                                                                 CIP

Book and cover design: Christopher Dean

10   9   8   7   6   5   4   3   2   1

Distributed in Canada by
Raincoast Books
112 East Third Avenue
Vancouver, B.C. V5T 1C8

Chronicle Books
275 Fifth Street
San Francisco, California 94103

HEMINGWAY'S SPAIN

INTRODUCTION

BY BARNABY CONRAD

One day, in the spring of 1971, I telephoned from my home in San Francisco to my old friend Loomis Dean, *Life* magazine's chief photographer in Paris.

"Loomis," I said over the crackling phone, "drop everything. I have a great job for you!"

"When?"

"Starts tomorrow, for a week, and—"

"Couldn't possibly, old boy." His mellifluous voice always sounds to me like an Englishman reared in New Orleans. "You see, I have this really important assignment in Monaco and—"

"But this will be fantastic! The same people who promoted the Frazier-Ali fight!"

"Impossible, I'm afraid," he said. "Princess Grace and Rainier are—"

"These promoters are putting on what they're billing as the bullfight of the century! Starring El Cordobés, first corrida ever shown on TV via Telstar all over the world, and they want you to photograph it and me to narrate it!"

Silence. "Where?"

"Jaen," I said.

"Spain?" he said. "Jaen, *Spain?*"

"Spain!" I said.

The pause from Paris was Wagnerian but brief. "I think," he drawled, and I pictured him looking at his Patek Philippe, "I think I can still catch the 3:45 to Madrid."

So Ernest Hemingway, Loomis Dean, and I have something profound in common—a deep and abiding love for Spain. This book captures in photographs some of the essence of that enigmatic, contradictory, and provocative country, a land whose contagion compelled Hemingway to write short stories and novels that many consider his best work. It is an attempt to make Hemingway's Spain, if not Hemingway himself, live again.

Loomis Dean, whose photographs have served for some fifty *Life* magazine covers (including the famous one of Hemingway on the back cover of this book), was assigned to record what proved to be Hemingway's final visit to Spain in 1960. But before and after that trip, Loomis made dozens of forays from his Paris base into the Iberian Peninsula, and always with his cameras slung around his neck, ready to capture the telling image. A selection of the results appears in this book, culled and organized with loving care by his son, Christopher Dean. Some of these photographs were taken years after Hemingway's death; indeed several recall that memorable Jaen assignment in 1971. But all contain a certain *simpatía* and *empatía* for Spain, its culture, its people, its festivals, its landscape, expressed as we feel Hemingway might have perceived them.

Those who may cavil about

Castles abound in Spain, but none are as castle-like as that in Segovia . Episodes of *For Whom the Bell Tolls* took place near here.

the preponderance of bullfighting photographs must accept that Spain and tauromachy were one to Hemingway; to him, the ethos of the Spanish people, their bravery, their arrogance, their quixotism, their love of gallantry, was embodied in the anachronistic taurine ritual. As the Spanish historian Cossío points out in his series of encyclopedic volumes, *Los Toros*, there is no ramification of Spanish culture, no social, commercial, or artistic aspect or endeavor that is not touched and influenced by bullfighting. Hemingway was ever sensitive to that, even to the point of using bullfighting terms to define military action during that country's civil war.

Long before I ever went there, I fell in love with Spain through Hemingway's writings; *Death in the Afternoon* changed my life, shaped my life, and almost cost me my life. I read it when I was seventeen and was so struck by his vision of bullfighting that as soon as possible I tucked the book under my arm and headed to Mexico, the nearest place that had bullfights. I was infatuated with the colors, the capework, the music, the pageantry of the corrida, and the paintings that suggested themselves throughout the spectacle. But, like most Americans, I thought it was cruel and declared that the bull had no chance.

I quickly learned that although the bull had about as much chance of survival as a Swift and Armour candidate in Chicago, he did have many an opportunity to collect his opponent during the hot-blooded fifteen-minute encounter, and that most matadors were gored many, many times during their careers, sometimes fatally. And while cruel, it was not as cruel as rodeos, where the livestock is abused over and over again; or zoos, where the inhabitants are imprisoned for a lifetime; or even deer or fox hunting, where, unlike the bull, the quarry is terrified. It is certainly not to be compared to the ultimate cruelty to animals, the leg-trapping of fur-bearing creatures for the vanity of the fashionable of the world. Bullfighting was indefensible perhaps—but irresistible.

Furthermore, I thought it looked easy, and one day in Mexico City, using my raincoat as a cape, I jumped down into the ring, landing directly in the middle of the action. One charge from the fright-ening half-ton of horned black fury convinced me I had been wrong in my assessment, and I dove ignominiously over the fence.

The real bullfighters were amused by this gringo's presumption and invited me out to the ranches to learn about the extraordinarily difficult science of making a bull go from point A to point B with elegance and grace and without getting one's thorax bisected. How felicitous Hemingway's phrase, "grace under pressure"!

Three months later I was badly injured by a bull and returned to the States on crutches. In 1943 I was graduated from Yale, went into the Foreign Service, and was assigned to Vigo in north-western Spain as an American vice-consul.

Vigo was not the Spain with which Hemingway had seduced me, the colorful, gypsified Iberia I had dreamed of. It was a stark and gray and dull port city, and only the impounded Nazi submarine and its crew held any of the drama and excitement for which I yearned. But six weeks later I was transferred to Seville, the heart of the country, the land of Carmen, flamenco, guitars, carriages, brave bulls and brazen women, and all the other clichés associated with Spain. It was all true, just as Hemingway had described it, and I was in heaven.

Hemingway himself, of course,

Journalist Charles Wertenbaker observed in 1944 that Hemingway was as possessive about bulls and bullfighting as ever—as "if he had staked out a personal claim which others could invade at their peril." And the bullfight was as active in his creative imagination as ever.

was not in Spain in those years, but I met many of the matadors he had written about — the mercurial bald gypsy El Gallo, the green-eyed charmer Cagancho, and the majestic Marcial Lalanda. Manolete and Arruza became my friends. They were real! I even knew Cayetano Ordóñez, the inspiration for the young Pedro Romero in *The Sun Also Rises*. I would lunch with the colorful Sidney Franklin several times a week and listen to tales about him and Hemingway in the old days. (He merits an entire

chapter at the end of *Death in the Afternoon*.) That Sidney emerged as the hero of his every anecdote made them no less fascinating.

I began bullfighting again under the tutelage of the legendary Juan Belmonte, out on his great estate, and appeared on the same program with him in 1945, the most exciting day of my life. He was old then, fifty-six, but full of a renewed love of bullfighting. It was marvelous to be with him and to see him perform like a young man. As Hemingway wrote: "The cynical

ones are the best companions. But the best of all are the cynical ones when they are still devout; or after; when having been devout, then cynical, they become devout again by cynicism. Juan Belmonte is an example of the last stage." (One day at the ranch Belmonte remarked to the renowned matadora, Conchita Cintrón, "Ah, yes, Hemingway — that man with the face of a lion and the heart of a boy!" And wasn't it the great historian Salvador de Madariaga who declared: "America is a land of boys who refuse to

The Peralta Ranch and its owner embodied the Spain Hemingway loved, a world of horses and bulls and male pride.

grow up"?)

As an amateur, I fought many times in Spain and three times in Lima, Peru. In 1958 I performed for the last time near Madrid, was gored almost fatally, and, with a sigh of both relief and sadness, "cut the pigtail."

Since then I've returned to the Iberian Peninsula a dozen times, drawn back to Spain again and again like Hemingway and Loomis Dean, always encountering different and fascinating aspects of the country.

Ernest Hemingway began his love affair with Spain the way I did — and at about the same age — by going to Vigo first. Except for a brief stop at Algeciras in 1919, when he was twenty and returning home from Italy after being wounded in the war, Hemingway's introduction to Spain was Vigo. It was 1921 and he and Hadley had just been married and were on their way to Paris to begin their life together. In a letter to his parents from the ship, he tells them how hot it is for December, and of the great schools of tuna in the harbor. (His greatest enthusiasm, however, was reserved for recounting the details of a match he had had on board with a professional boxer and how he had him on the verge of a knockout.)

But Vigo stayed in his mind, Spain nagged at him, and he read all he could about the country and its customs, especially *tauromaquia.*

Sidney Franklin showed Hemingway the inside world of bullfighting, and here they are at the height of both their careers.

In Paris he wrote his first piece on bullfighting without ever having seen one; it appeared as a vignette in *The Little Review* and in it he described the death of a matador, based mainly on what he had heard from his painter friend Mike Strater and Gertrude Stein. He longed to see a real corrida though, and finally went with two friends to Madrid to his first bullfight, a *novillada,* in the spring of 1923. He became an instant aficionado and afterward could talk of little else but the courage of the men and the bulls. He said repeatedly that people were wrong to call bullfighting brutal, that every corrida was a great and wonderful tragedy.

That spring he turned into a bullfight fanatic. He traveled around Andalusia, following the matadors. He loved Granada, with its gypsies and corrida traditions, and, best of all, the small but spectacular town of Ronda, the "cradle of bullfighting." The night life of Seville and flamenco dancing bored him. "Oh for Christ's sake," he kept saying, "more flamingos!" But the bulls never bored him.

When he returned to Paris he longed for Spain. Gertrude Stein told him about Pamplona and urged him to attend. Hadley, pregnant, was eager to go and both agreed that the bullfights might be a "stalwart prenatal influence" for the baby. Ernest, by now obsessed with *la fiesta brava,* could hardly

The caretaker of the Linares arena enjoys showing aficionados the fatal spot where Islero and Manolete killed each other in 1947, a most Hemingwayesque and Spanish tragedy.

wait for July and the fiestas of San Fermín to begin.

Pamplona was no letdown. Hadley and Ernest rose at dawn to watch the bulls and steers run down the street in pursuit of dozens of *pamplonicas* in costume and in varying states of drunkenness. Those same bulls would be fought in the afternoon by Spain's top matadors. And so it went for the whole wild week. Ernest was particularly impressed with the cape-work of Nicanor Villalta, "the Aragon Telephone Pole," and he and Hadley agreed to name their child, if a son, after him. (John Nicanor Hadley Hemingway once remarked to me: "How could any kid named after Nicanor Villalta and with Gertrude Stein as his god-mother possibly go wrong?")

Hemingway had never been happier. Back in Paris he wrote an enthusiastic letter to old friend and fellow World War I ambulance driver William Horne, Jr.:

... have just got back from the best week I ever had since the Section—the big Feria at Pamplona—5 days of bull fighting dancing all day and all night—wonderful music—drums, reed pipes, fifes—faces of Velásquez's drinkers, Goya and Greco faces, all the men in blue shirts and red handkerchiefs circling lifting floating dance. We [are] the only foreigners at the damn fair. Every morning the bulls that are going to fight that

afternoon released from the corrals at the far side of town and race through the long main street of the town to the bull ring with all of the young bucks of Pamplona running ahead of them! A mile and a half run — all the side streets barred off with big wooden gates and all this gang going like hell with the bulls trying to get them.

By God they have bull fights in that town! There were 8 of the best toreros in Spain and 5 of them got gored! The bulls bagged just one a day.

Though he had written before of bullfights, in November 1924, after weeks of work, Hemingway finished a masterpiece; *The Undefeated* is one of the author's greatest stories and certainly the finest ever written on the corrida. In 1926 it appeared in his short story collection *Men Without Women*, which caused almost as much of a literary sensation as his first anthology, *In Our Time*, had the year before.

Now more than ever, Hemingway was fiercely possessive of his knowledge and love of Spain. He felt he'd discovered it and bullfighting and wanted all the world to know about it. When Dorothy Parker visited there in 1926 and then returned to Paris, she let Hemingway know how much she "hated the damn country." So offended was Hemingway that he wrote a long, vile poem about her, she who was

his longtime and steadfast admirer. Part of it goes:

But you loved dogs and other people's children / and hated Spain where they are cruel to donkeys. / Hoping the bulls would kill the matadors.

With Hemingway, if you didn't like Spain there wasn't much else he wanted to talk to you about.

Out of his fascination with the country, bullfighting, and the ancient ritual of Pamplona came what many believe is Hemingway's finest novel. He began writing it on July 21, 1925, in Valencia, and sent off the finished manuscript to Scribners on April 24, 1926, from Paris.

The Sun Also Rises evolved out of a trip to Pamplona made early in July 1925 with his wife Hadley and a disparate group, American and English, and the effect of the annual, week-long San Fermín fiesta upon them. He had attended the 1923 and 1924 fiestas, always staying at the Hotel Quintana (Hotel Montoya in the novel), and the owner, Juanito Quintana, who introduced him to Maera and the other matadors, became his great friend and mentor in the bull world. In 1925 Cayetano Ordóñez, whose *nom de taureau* was Niño de la Palma, after his home district in the town of Ronda, was the new idol of Spain and had captured the attention of Hemingway as well: "He was the best-looking boy I ever

Three principals in the Pamplona drama, out of which came *The Sun Also Rises*. The year is 1925. Left to right: Hemingway, Lady Duff Twysden, and Hadley Hemingway.

saw." He makes him "nineteen or twenty" in *The Sun Also Rises*, but Ordóñez was actually twenty-one years old and had been a full matador only one month. Already he was being hailed as the successor to the legendary Joselito, who had been fatally gored in 1920 at the age of twenty-five. Adding to the excitement was the return to the ring of Juan Belmonte, who had retired shortly after the shocking death of his friend and rival.

That July in Pamplona, Cayetano Ordóñez was out to show the world that Belmonte was through and that he was the new king of the rings. On the way to the fiesta, Hemingway had told his traveling companions about the exciting Ordóñez; he had seen him in Madrid the day of his presentation, and in Valencia watched admiringly as he did "two faenas that were so beautiful and wonderful that I can remember them pass by pass today. He was sincerity and

purity of style itself. . . ."

Hemingway's hard-drinking group fell into the spirit of Pamplona with gusto, swept Ordóñez into their orbit, and embraced the handsome young matador— literally, in the case of Lady Duff Twysden; she would become Lady Brett, of the wanderlust and wandering lust, in the novel already germinating in Hemingway's head.

(Niño de la Palma died, in Madrid, an impoverished drunk, a few months after Ernest Hemingway's death. Lady Duff—born Mary Smurthwaite—died in 1938 at the age of forty-six, in Santa Fe, New Mexico.)

The Sun Also Rises, published in 1926, brought Hemingway critical acclaim and international renown. It also put Pamplona on the map for all time. Has any American writer stamped his or her imprimatur on a foreign place with quite the impact that this short novel did? In the heart of Pamplona today, and quite rightly so, a large bust of Hemingway is prominently displayed; what was a small, strictly Spanish village tradition has burgeoned into a nightmarish tourist carnival. When my son arrived in 1972 to run before the bulls, virtually half the people were non-Spanish tourists and the hotel rooms had been taken for months. Hemingway himself, when he saw it almost thirty years after writing *The Sun Also Rises*, was aghast at what he had wrought.

But in 1927, with Pauline Pfeiffer as his new wife, he thought the fair as wonderful as ever. They went on to San Sebastian, followed the bullfights to Valencia, and ended up in La Coruña, "a grand town as far out in the old Atlantic as Europe can get . . . [with] fine wide streets with no sidewalks or gutters and the first good food I've had all summer." And the nearby cathedral town of Santiago de Compostela was to Hemingway "the loveliest town in Spain."

Next to bullfighting, Hemingway loved the art of Spain, and he spent days at a time in the labyrinthine galleries of the Prado. He admired Spanish architecture also and made special forays to cities and towns with cathedrals of unusual interest. He was enamored with the countryside around Madrid and Santander and San Sebastian, and his idea of paradise was a picnic *al fresco español*, returning in time for a corrida, then drinks in a modest cantina to rehash the performances with the local experts.

In 1929 he met the brash twenty-six-year-old Brooklyn-born matador Sidney Franklin, né Frumpkin. After a taurine apprenticeship in Mexico, where he had originally gone to study painting, Franklin made his first appearance that June as a *novillero* in Spain in the prestigious arena of Seville. It was a total triumph, partly because of the novelty of his nationality, and partly because of his bravery and unexpected skill.

Franklin went on to fight thirteen more times that season—not many for a top *novillero*, but the corridas were in important cities and for large purses. Hemingway, determined to learn all he could about *la fiesta brava* with the idea of eventually doing a book, attached himself to Franklin's team and toured Spain with him. Fifteen years later in Seville, Sidney Franklin told me that at first he had no idea that Hemingway was a famous writer, even though *A Farewell to Arms* was shortly to become a runaway best seller. Sidney, highly intelligent but a nonreader, insisted

that he thought Hemingway was just another ardent hanger-on, tolerated him, and that it was some weeks before he learned exactly who his new friend was. (It should be said that Sidney Franklin was a delightful companion but was full of braggadocio and had only a nodding acquaintance with veracity.)

After having lived among the bullfighters and witnessed some fifteen hundred corridas, Hemingway finished his book. He also claimed to have read or perused 2,077 volumes on the lore and science of bullfighting before turning in the final manuscript of *Death in the Afternoon*, which was published in 1932. The reviews were mixed in

America, though the work certainly is the most eloquent explanation of the arcane spectacle ever written. In a letter to Hemingway, the editor Max Perkins wrote, "The book piles upon you wonderfully, and becomes to one reading it— who at first thinks bullfighting only a small matter—immensely important." Arnold Gingrich, founding editor of *Esquire*, declared the title the most provocative four-word poem in the English language.

Though some critics attacked *Death in the Afternoon*, they could not deny that Hemingway's love of Spain and its traditions shines through on almost every page. Nor could they ignore some fine, writerly prose, such as his passage on why killing the cowardly but superbly graceful and popular El Gallo "would be bad taste and prove the bullfight was wrong, not morally but aesthetically. . . . Do you know the sin it would be to ruffle the arrangement of the feathers on a hawk's neck if they could never be replaced as they were? Well, that would be the sin it would be to kill El Gallo."

In November 1933, after a summer spent in the Spanish heat, Pauline and Ernest went to Africa on safari and a new passion took hold of him. But he didn't lose touch with Spain.

The new republic established in 1931 had failed to meet Hemingway's expectations for

Hemingway, in the *Capea* that traditionally follows each morning running of the bulls in Pamplona, is directly in front of the horns, dressed in white pants. The animal has gored a Spaniard and seems about to collect his first American novelist.

reform, leaving him increasingly dismayed by a growing bureaucracy and a peasantry as poor as ever. A return to power by conservative forces in the 1933 elections troubled him more, however. The future looked hopeful with the Republican victory in 1936, only the rejoicing was to be short-lived.

Civil war soon broke out and Hemingway was both saddened and vitally interested; after all, the men on both sides were Spaniards, and it was often brother against brother as it had been in the American Civil War. He sent a personal donation of forty thousand

The historian Ganivet states, "Every Spanish military leader, from El Cid and Gonzalo de Cordoba to the more recent leaders of Spanish civil strife, has been a roving king, a warrior, master of his own fate, responsible to no one, and accepting no dictate save that of his own conscience."

An Andaluz peasant, straight from the pages of *For Whom the Bell Tolls.*

dollars to the Spanish Republicans for ambulances and medicine; from the beginning he had regarded the other side as a fascist movement akin to Italy's Fascists.

He didn't claim to know much about politics, but he wrote his mother-in-law that even if "the Reds" were as bad as they were rumored to be, they still represented the people of the country "as against the absentee landlords, the Moors, the Italians and the Germans." Hemingway added that he knew very well that most of "the whites" were also "rotten." He thought the war very important and felt that it would affect everyone ultimately, since it was so clearly a "dress rehearsal for the inevitable European War."

Even less political was Sidney Franklin; I remember his telling me that Hemingway had phoned

him early in 1937 saying: "Pack up. February 27 we're going to the war in Spain!"

"Great!" Sid answered. "Which side are we on?"

Hemingway went to the

Salvador de Madariaga observed that Hemingway "developed roots in Iberian soil," that he was "inside Spain, living her life," and that he may "well have been the non-Spaniard who . . . has come closest to penetrating her soul."

In the late 1950s, John Huston and Hemingway agreed that it was good to be back in "the last wonderful country."

Iberian Peninsula as a war correspondent for the North American Newspaper Alliance attached to the Loyalist Army. He and Franklin arrived in Barcelona and headed directly for the front at Guadalajara where the Italian forces were suffering a humiliating defeat. (To this day Spaniards, when referring to the speed of anything, use the phrase "faster than the Italians ran at Guadalajara!") They then traveled to Madrid and set up their headquarters in the Hotel Florida, which was home to the foreign press. In April Hemingway covered the great Republican offensive at University City and the Nationalist counteroffensive, during which Madrid was heavily bombarded for twelve days. More than thirty shells fell on the Hotel Florida.

When not filing stories, Hemingway was busy hunting up food for the wounded; he even resorted to shooting rabbits in the park and wangling caviar from the Russians, who were helping the Republican cause.

He returned to America to raise money for ambulances for the Republicans and, as much as he hated public speaking, gave a lecture at Carnegie Hall on the dangers of fascism. Back in Spain, he met and fell in love with another correspondent, Martha Gellhorn (whom he would take for his third wife in the fall of 1940).

After his fifth wartime trip to

Spain and the Republicans' retreat from the Ebro and defeat in Cataluña, Hemingway realized the cause was lost; he left Spain, disappointed and disillusioned.

He took up residence in Cuba in 1939 and dedicated himself to writing *For Whom the Bell Tolls*. The locale is a Loyalist guerrilla camp in the Sierra de Guadarrama range northwest of Madrid, the hero a young idealist from Montana, and his assignment is to blow up a strategic bridge. At one point, Hemingway has his hero, Robert Jordan, say about Spaniards: "There is no finer and no worse people in the world."

The book was an unqualified success, critically and financially, and sold to Paramount Pictures for the highest price ever paid for a novel at that time. Its author was delighted when his friends Gary Cooper and Ingrid Bergman were cast as the leads.

For many years Hemingway boycotted Spain, vowing to stay away "until Franco released all my friends who were political prisoners." Finally, he felt comfortable enough to go back.

It was 1953, and he relived his youth by returning to Pamplona for the fiesta, by trout fishing in the Irati and seeing many bullfights. Only now his wife was not Hadley,

she was Mary Welsh, and he had a gray beard, and the bullfighter was not Niño de la Palma, but rather his son, Antonio Ordóñez. The passing of time seems not to have diminished Hemingway's love for either the country or the bulls, and he joyously proclaimed Antonio Ordóñez a far better matador than his father on his best day. From Pamplona they drove to Sepúlveda, Segovia, and San Ildefonso so that Ernest could show Mary the settings he'd described in *For Whom the Bell Tolls*; they occupied the same room in the Hotel Florida that he had stayed in during the civil war.

Later that year they went to Africa and suffered two plane

Hemingway in Bill Davis's pool near Málaga, 1959, during "one of the happiest times of my life . . ."

Luis Miguel Dominguin, a bullfighter since he was 10 years old, observes the bull's initial charge in a corrida *mano a mano* with his brother-in-law Antonio Ordóñez.

crashes that caused innumerable injuries to Hemingway. He never totally recovered. Nevertheless, in 1954, the year he won the Nobel Prize, Hemingway showed up in Madrid for the San Isidro bullfights; returning again in 1955, he continued to be impressed by Antonio Ordóñez's skill in the arena.

Hemingway declared 1959 to be one of his happiest years ever in Spain. Almost obsessional in his dedication and devotion to Ordóñez, he accompanied him on his exhausting corrida schedule to Madrid, Seville, Córdoba, Málaga, Ronda, Algeciras, Aranjuez, Valencia, Alicante, Zaragoza, Burgos, Barcelona, Vitoria, and Bilbao. Hemingway had agreed to do a long piece for *Life* magazine on the rivalry between the two top matadors of Spain, Dominguín and Ordóñez; Spain's *número uno*, Dominguín, was lured out of retirement, much as he himself had done to Manolete in 1947 when as a bold young matador he had challenged the old master in a series of fights that led to Manolete's death. Ordóñez and Dominguín happened to be brothers-in-law, Antonio being married to Carmen, Dominguín's beautiful sister. They were also friends, until the press whipped up the publicity about the showdown.

Back in Cuba Hemingway labored over *The Dangerous Summer*; from a simple magazine article it had ballooned into a huge sprawling book. He felt he must return to Spain for the final touches, so he went back to Madrid August 5, 1960, for his last visit. *Life* assigned Loomis Dean for several weeks to the Hemingway entourage.

"After all my varied and important assignments over the years I was surprised how thrilled I was with this one," related Loomis as we worked on this book. "Hemingway and Spain! As with so many other people, he had helped shape my feelings about this marvelous country. I was apprehensive. People had warned me that he was depressed, ill, and rather difficult, but I found him considerate and mostly happy—especially around the bullfighters and the arenas. It turned out to be a dream assign-

The beauty of the bullfight resides in the ballet of grace and fury performed by the matador and the bull.

Hemingway met Antonio Ordóñez in 1953, then saw him again in 1954, 1955, 1959, and lastly in 1960 when this photo was taken. "Better than his father on his best day," he stated.

a young American writer from Oak Park, Illinois, so many decades ago.

And as I myself turn the pages and look at the familiar scenes, I once again feel the heat of the Andalusia sun, smell the fresh strawberries at Aranjuez, hear Belmonte's breathy chuckle, tremble at the sound of huge hooves on Pamplona's cobblestones, see the golden sand found only in Seville's arena, feel my heart pound at the sight of the black-tipped ivory horns jutting from a bull's head, marvel at the magic that a mere magenta cloth and a man and a bull can produce, tap my feet to a wild *paso doble*, and remember the lost love of a beautiful *malagueña*.

ment, watching the author interact with the people and the country."

Yet after a few weeks in Spain Hemingway announced flatly that he feared "a complete physical and nervous crack-up from deadly overwork."

Early in October he returned to America, and in December entered the Mayo Clinic for treatment. He killed himself in his home in Ketchum, Idaho, in the early morning of July 2, 1961. He was sixty-two years old.

A few days before, he had sent a telegram to Pamplona cancelling

his hotel reservation for the fiesta and his reserved *barrera* seats in the bullring. One can only guess at the anguish this caused him, bidding his beloved Spain farewell forever.

What follows is Loomis Dean's splendid pictorial tribute to the unique and passionate country that Ernest Hemingway loved and that inspired some of his best writings. This carefully gleaned photographic collection forms a kaleidoscope of that "unspoiled and unbelievably tough and wonderful" place that captured the heart and fired the imagination of

Loomis Dean's photos in this final year show Hemingway at his happiest.

"There are no other countries like Spain," Robert Jordan said politely.

"You are right," Fernando said. "There is no other country in the world like Spain."

"Hast thou ever seen any other country?" the woman asked him.

"Nay," said Fernando. "Nor do I wish to."

— Hemingway,
For Whom The Bell
Tolls

O ne has to remind oneself that before Hemingway's beloved Spaniards there were Moors, and before the Moors the Romans, who began colonizing this splendid land around 200 B.C. There are more magnificent traces of the Roman epoch around Mérida, in the province of Badajoz, than anywhere else in Spain. From near this majestic aqueduct the conquistadores Cortés and Pizarro came. And not many miles away, in Cordoba, the noble Romans Hadrian, Trajan, and Seneca were born.

In the morning there we would have breakfast and then go out to swim . . . the water clear as light, and varying in temperature as you sunk down, cool, deep cool, cold, and the shade from the trees on the bank when the sun was hot, the ripe wheat in the wind up on the other side and sloping to the mountain. There was an old castle at the head of the valley where the river came out between two rocks; and we lay naked on the short grass in the sun and later in the shade.

—Hemingway,
Death in the
Afternoon

Then there was the smell of heather crushed and the roughness of the bent stalks under her head and the sun bright on her closed eyes . . . and for her everything was red, orange, gold-red from the sun on the closed eyes . . .

— For Whom The Bell Tolls

RETURN TO SPAIN

After Spain's civil war, Hemingway swore not to return to the Iberian Peninsula until Generalissimo Franco released all his friends who had been jailed as political prisoners.

It was fourteen years later — plus a world war, two books, a divorce, and new marriage — when the last of his friends was freed. He referred to that time as "like being in jail except that I was locked out; not locked in." He later said, "I had never expected to be allowed to return to the country that I loved more than any other except my own."

Here he is in 1960, his last visit to Spain, at La Consula, the Málaga estate of Nathan "Bill" Davis. An American with business

interests in Spain, Davis was the brother-in-law of the British critic Cyril Connolly and a collector of literary figures. He had joyfully accompanied Hemingway on the strenuous taurine hegira of the year before while the author was gathering material for the long *Life* magazine piece, "The Dangerous Summer." Hemingway came back the following August to finish the

three-part article, and Davis was appalled at the change in his friend: sleeplessness, worry, paranoia, and frustration from his memory failure bedeviled him.

Yet he had happy moments, as Loomis Dean's photographs show, and he was perhaps happier here than he could have been anywhere in the world, especially with the many adulators, the presence of

good Spanish food and wine, and the prospect of great bullfighting in the afternoon.

And there was a stand-up desk and a table that had been made especially for him.

"It was a wonderful place to work and I started working at once."

Hemingway felt at home in his old friend Davis's estate. It reminded him of his Cuban house except that it was larger, with formal gardens and a sixty-foot swimming pool. He had a spacious corner room with a balcony overlooking the beautiful garden.

"Anyone who couldn't write here couldn't write nowhere," Hemingway joked.

But he was increasingly aware of his failing powers, and his friends and family were worried.

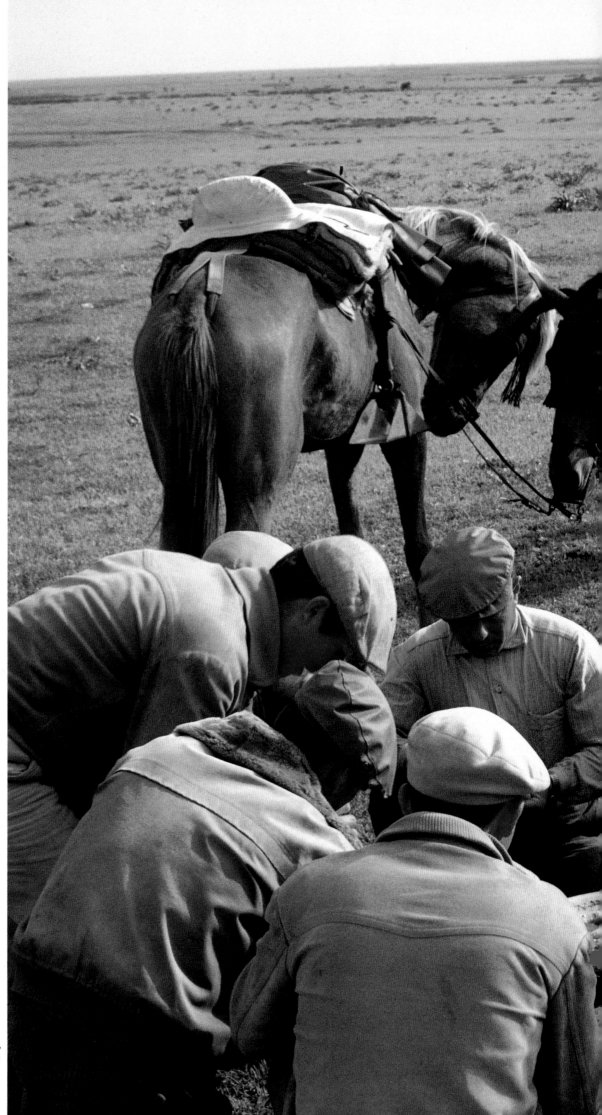

In Spain Hemingway found being practiced some things he believed in and he liked the bullfights and the people. And he rediscovered parts of America, especially the West, in Spain, which made him love Spain all the more and gave him common ground with the Spaniards who had discovered America.

—Allen Josephs, in
*Hemingway
Review*, 1988

The Peralta ranch,
Seville

Hemingway was fascinated by the people of Spain, the extraordinary visages of the ordinary men and women. He agreed with Gerald Brenan who once wrote:

"... we look at the passing faces, so lovely or so deeply marked—either preternaturally solemn with the leaden solemnity of Spaniards or else more than usually gay and animated. The bald are more bald, the obese more obese, the thin more cadaverous, the one-legged more limbless than in other countries."

Hemingway and Belmonte, considered the inventor of modern bullfighting, were not good friends, but they were important to each other in different ways. Belmonte figures prominently at the end of *The Sun Also Rises*, mostly as a foil; in the novel, as in life, he had come out of retirement after the death of his arch rival and friend, the incomparable Joselito, and Hemingway uses Belmonte's tired, cynical routine greatness in the arena, as a contrast to the fresh talented handsome Pedro Romero with whom Lady Brett falls in love. (Romero was based on Cayetano Ordóñez, called Niño de la Palma, and Brett on Lady Duff Twysden.)

In *Death in the Afternoon*, Belmonte is constantly referred to as being one of the greatest bullfighters of all time.

I once asked Belmonte about Hemingway, and he wrinkled his brow and his great jaw jutted out and he said in his lifelong stammer: "I believe I met him t-t-twice. Once in P-Pamplona. I can't remember where the other t-time was. A great w-writer."

In July of 1961, a friend told me of coming across Belmonte at a sidewalk cafe in Seville. He was sitting with the newspaper reporting Hemingway's suicide across his lap, reading it over and over.

"Isn't that terrible?" remarked the friend.

"Not at all," said Belmonte. "The glories were past for him. It was time."

Several months later, five days before his 70th birthday, Belmonte remarked to the same friend: "There are only three things in life that I still like to do—make love, ride horses, and fight bulls, and my doctor has forbidden me all of them. I should like to die doing one of those things."

The next day, Sunday, after attending mass, Belmonte paid a visit to his mistress, then drove out to his great estate in the country where he raised fighting bulls and olives. He had his favorite horse saddled, rode out into the fields, and, one after another, caped some seven animals. When exhausted, he returned to the house, wrote a short note saying that no one was to be blamed for his death, and then shot himself.

His funeral was one of the grandest ever witnessed in Seville; his coffin was paraded around the bull ring, the site of so many of his triumphs, and he was buried next to the tomb of Joselito.

Belmonte . . . was a genius, who could break the rules of bullfighting and could torear, that is the only word for all the actions performed by a man with the bull, as it was known to be impossible to torear. Once he had done it, all bull-fighters had to do it, or attempt to do it since there is no going back in the matter of sensations . . . He did not accept any rules made without testing whether they might be broken, and he was a genius and a great artist. The way Belmonte worked was not a heritage, nor a development; it was a revolution.

— Death in the Afternoon

Fighting bulls are bred like race-horses, some of the oldest breeding establishments being several hundred years old. A good bull is worth about $2,000. They are bred for speed, strength and viciousness. In other words a good fighting bull is an absolutely incorrigible bad bull.

—"Bull Fighting a Tragedy"
Hemingway, *The Toronto Star Weekly:* October 1923

Never was a century more disastrous to a nation than the nineteenth century was to Spain.

So she limped into our own times—with one half of her being, for the other half was still lingering wistfully with the Cid and the conquistadores. She was a mess of a country: addled by bitter politics at home—between 1814 and 1923 there were forty-three *coups d'etat*; embroiled in constant wars in the pathetic remnants of her empire, now confined to a few sandy or foetid enclaves in Africa; diplomatically a cipher, strategically so inessential that the First World War contemptuously passed her by. Conflicting ideologies tortured her—dogmas of monarchy, theocracy, despotism, democracy, socialism, anarchism, Communism. Her rural poverty and urban squalor periodically erupted into violence. Her colonial policies were so inept that in 1921 her Moroccan army was annihilated in the Rif. A dictator, Primo de Rivera, came and went; in 1931 the last of the Bourbons, bowing himself out of the chaos, gave way to a left-wing Republic; and in 1936 all these centuries of failure, schism, and frustration gave birth to that ultimate despair, the Spanish Civil War.

It was theoretically a revolt by the Nationalist conservatives against the Republic, but in the end it was really a double revolution—by Right and Left against Centre. The passions it brought so hideously to the boil had been simmering for five centuries, and were so wounding that to this day the scars still show.

— James Morris, in
The Presence of Spain

The Falangista Salute, an anathema to Hemingway

Franco and his Cuadrilla

A convert to Catholicism, Hemingway declared in a letter from Spain in 1938 that the only way he could run his life decently was to accept the discipline of the Church, but the problem was that the Church had sided with the enemy, i.e., Franco's forces. This fact bothered him so much that he even quit praying, for it somehow seemed "crooked" to have anything to do with a religious institution so closely allied to fascism.

Although his faith was shaken, in 1959 he nevertheless told another convert, Gary Cooper, that he "still believed in belief."

Spain is a Christian country in the way that Saudi Arabia is Muslim, Burma Buddhist, or Russia Communist. To the average citizen of the West, with his pagan or humanist social background, her Christianity is as exotically mysterious as any faith of fetish or of ancestry. It is not merely that the State is officially Christian: in Spain every aspect of life is governed by the fact of Christianity, and the moment you set foot within her frontiers the tokens of the creed are as ubiquitous as prayer-wheels in Nepal, or prayer-mats in Arabia. Christianity is the binding force of this centrifugal nation. It was in the name of Christ that the Catholic Monarchs united Spain, earning for this country, by Papal Bull, the perpetual right to eat meat on Fridays. In a sculptured relief in Granada Cathedral Ferdinand and Isabel are shown accepting the surrender of Granada with their spiritual adviser, Cardinal Mendoza, so powerful a prelate that he was known as Tertius Rex; and it is properly symbolic, perhaps, that of the three, only the Cardinal is wearing gloves. It was in the cause of Christian unity that the Jews and the Moors were expelled—the Jews because of their 'continual attempts to divert and turn faithful Christians from our holy Catholic faith, taking them away from it and drawing them towards their own diseased belief and opinions.' The ships of the conquistadores crossed the Atlantic loaded deep with crosses, missionaries, missals, and Christian convictions, and Spain in her heyday saw herself as the champion of Christian orthodoxy, whose task it was to unite the world in Catholicism; it was the defeat of the Armada by the English Protestants, in 1588, that cracked her confidence in her mission and herself.

In the Spanish context Christianity has always meant power and purpose.

— James Morris, in
The Presence of
Spain

The famous *fallas* festival
of Valencia

H emingway said that he always had more faith than knowledge of his religion, but he was a Catholic, though often a wavering or exasperated one. He was continuously fascinated by how large a part religion played in the makeup of the Spaniard and the history of the country.

— James Morris, in
*The Presence of
Spain*

The castles of Spain seem to be an integral part of the landscape, rising out of the earth like exotic rock formations.

For one must admit that the earthiness of Spain, which is the cousin of backwardness, is often very beautiful to see. This is a society poised still in the attitudes that characterized us all, before the machine came to shift our rhythms. One of the glories of Spain is her bread, which the Romans remarked upon a thousand years ago, and which is said to be so good because the corn is left to the last possible moment to ripen upon the stalk. It is the best bread I know, and its coarse, strong, springy substance epitomizes all that is admirable about Spanish simplicity. It is rough indeed, and unrefined, but feels full of life; and poor Spain too, as you may see her in Andalusia, seems crude but richly organic. Most of her vast landscapes have still never felt the tread of a tractor. All has been tilled by hand, and all still feels ordered and graceful, the energies of the earth rising in logi-

cal gradation through ear of corn or trunk of olive into the walls and crowning towers of the villages, sprouting themselves like outcrops of rock from the soil. Spain is a hierarchical country: on the farm, from the grave old paterfamilias at one end to the turnips in the field at the other; in the nation, from the grandees of Church and State, the brilliant young men at the Feria, or the debutantes showing their knees in the noisy sports cars of Madrid, to those simple people of the thatched huts, with their huddle of blankets on the earth floor, and their piglets in sacks beside the fire. It may not be just, the *sol y sombra*, it is inevitably changing, but it feels all too natural: just as the bread, though it may lack finesse, certainly fills you up.

— James Morris, in *The Presence of Spain*

oth in Hemingway's time and now, bullfighters live hard, fast—and very well. Here is Jaime Ostos's car, with the capes and swords packed on top, en route to the next arena at the height of the taurine season.

So I wired Carmen we would be there in the morning and sent messages from all of us. Bill's theory was that Spanish roads in spite of the dangerous curves and drops and the four mountain ranges we had to cross were safer to drive at night because there was almost no cart traffic and no herds on the roads and almost no private cars.

—Hemingway,
The Dangerous
Summer

En route to Granada

*S*tarting out to drive in a part of the country you do not know, the distances all seem longer than they are, the difficult parts of the road much worse than it is, the dangerous curves more dangerous and the steep ascents have a greater percentage of grade. It is like going back into your childhood or early youth.

—The Dangerous Summer

The rest of us headed for Alicante, then through date palms and the rich, crowded, flat farming and fruit country of Murcia, past Lorca, to break out and up into the wild mountain country and along the lonely valleys with the white-washed houses of the villages and the herds of sheep and goats raising the dust along the road until we came down out of the hills in the dark past the entry to the ravine where they had shot Federico Garcia Lorca and saw the lights of Granada.

— The Dangerous Summer

On the road to Hemingway's favorite town—Ronda

It would be quiet in San Sebastian. There was a fine beach there.

—Hemingway,
The Sun Also
Rises

Franco's yacht sits in the harbor of San Sebastian.

San Sebastian

I *walked around the harbour and out along the promenade.*

—The Sun Also Rises

On the afternoon of May 30, 1959, Hemingway and his bull-following entourage stopped at Aranjuez, a town just south of Madrid famous for its asparagus and strawberries:

"The rain was gone," he wrote, "and the town was new-washed in the sun. We went to the old cafe-restaurant under the shade of trees and watched the [Tajo] river and the excursion boats."

Excessive in everything, Hemingway's love of Spanish food and wine crept into most of his writings about Spain.

He also knew and loved the Spaniards for their arrogance and independence. As Laurie Lee wrote in 1975:

"But within the bright walls of its [Spain's] towns and villages it has developed a gregarious and extrovert ritual of life in which there are few outsiders and little loneliness. The Spaniard believes himself superior, both in culture and morality, to any other people in the world, and believes this so steadfastly he neither boasts nor hates but welcomes strangers with a chivalrous warmth based on compassion for their benighted shortcomings."

Málaga

Málaga was Hemingway's base in 1959 while writing **The Dangerous Summer,** and where he had his elaborate sixtieth birthday party.

He wrote to his son Patrick, "This place where we stay is really lovely . . . it is like everything was in the old days before they spoiled everything."

Hemingway's love of Spain and things Spanish was most fervent when it came to the paintings of Velásquez, Goya, and Miró, rather than the country's music and dance. At first he knew and cared little about flamenco, referring to it derisively as "flamingo." Later he came to appreciate the wild and basic poetry inherent in the folk songs and *cante jondo,* the deep singing of the gypsies that to the untutored ear can sound like the tortured victims of Torquemada. Most of the songs are sad, anguished expressions of loneliness and despair, like this *soleares:*

Sometimes I would like
to go mad and not feel,
for being mad takes away grief,
grief that has no solution.
Death came to my bedside
but did not wish to take me,
as my destiny was not complete;
on its departure I began to weep.
I am living in the world

devoid of hope;
it is not necessry to bury me,
as I am buried alive.

There is a distinct Arab flavor to the music due to the seven-centuries-long occupation of southern Spain by the Moors, and perhaps even to the liturgical chants of the medieval Jews. Gypsy refugees from India in the mid-fifteenth century added their own interpretations.

How this kind of music and dance came to be called flamenco is not known for sure. The word means "Flemish," and some say it was born of the boisterous behavior of the Flanders court members who accompanied Charles V to Spain in 1517. Others say it got its name because the exaggerated postures of the dancers resembled flamingos, which *flamenco* also means. Perhaps Hemingway was right.

*S*panish women were literally born to dance. I remember seeing a friend's one-year-old daughter trying to totter through the steps of a **sevillana,** *the traditional carnation scotch-taped to her nearly bald head.*

La Chunga, one of Spain's oldest and most durable flamenco dancers, says: "When I dance, I am in a cloud. Sometimes it is a sad cloud. But if I am happy, I dance to show my happiness."

And even today, one can be a flamenco without being a musician or a dancer. It is an attitude toward life of which the music is but one manifestation. To "proper" society, flamenco came to mean a type of person who was emotionally uninhibited, more concerned with grasping the pleasure of the moment than with industriousness, and who often resided on the edge of the law. To the flamenco, it is a term of honor which marks a person who treasures freedom of movement over acquisition of property, and individual spontaneity and depth of expression over routine.

—Julian Gray

Nowhere else can romantic Spain, commercialized or not, be seen so readily as at Seville's annual spring fair. It has none of Pamplona's dangerous drunken rowdyism that Hemingway celebrated and enjoyed. James Morris, in a passage from *The Presence of Spain*, captures the spirit of this renowned *feria*:

It is part a parade, of horses, fashions, and handsome citizens. It is part a binge, where people eat and drink all night, and dance into the morning. It is part an entertainment, where the best dancers and musicians of Andalusia come to display their talents. It is part a mating session, where the best families gather to share reminiscences, swap prejudices, and introduce eligible nephews to likely nieces. In the morning there takes place the most brilliant of all Spain's paseos—*a paseo with horses.*

Hour after hour, in the warm spring sunshine, the Andalusians ride up and down that fairground—to see and be seen, look each other's dressage up and down, and inquire after the dear Marquis. The married and the very young ride by in lovely polished carriages, drawn sometimes by the proudest of mules, sometimes by pairs of elegant Arabs, and just occasionally by that prodigy of the carriage trade, a five-in-hand. Their coachmen are sometimes

decked up in gorgeous liveries, turbans, toppers, Druse costume or tam-o'-shanters, and often some winsome grand-daughter perches herself upon the open hood of the barouche, her frilled white skirt drooping over the back.

As for those of marriageable age, they trot up and down those boulevards like figures of Welsh mythology: two to a horse, the young man proud as a peacock in front, the girl seductively side-saddle behind. He is dressed in all the splendour of the Andalusian dandy, the tightest of jackets and the most rakish of hats, looking lithe, lean, and possibly corseted; she wears a rose in her hair and a long, full, flowing, flounced polka-dot dress — blue, pink, mauve, bright yellow or flaming red. Never was there such a morning spectacle. The old people look marvellously well fed and valeted; the coachmen are superbly cock-sure; and sometimes one of those court-ing couples will wheel around with a spark of hoofs, the beau reining sharply in like a cowboy at the brink of a can-yon, the belle clutching his shapely waist or holding the flower in her hair, to mount the pavement to some gay pavil-ion, the horse snorting and the lovers laughing, and accept a stirrup cup from a smiling friend.

La feria de Sevilla — an equine cocktail party

PAMPLONA!

Every year, beginning traditionally at the seventh hour of the seventh day of the seventh month, the town of Pamplona, located in the northeast corner of Spain in the Basque province of Navarra—goes totally insane.

Long before Hemingway discovered the Fiesta of San Fermín, Pamplonicas had been running through the streets in front of the bulls in the morning and drinking and dancing in the streets all night, shouting "riau, riau" and hitting each other with inflated bladders. In fact, Fermín, a third-century bishop who was martyred, became the patron saint of the town at the end of the sixteenth century when a plague that was ravaging the area disappeared after his name was invoked. The religious celebration to San Fermín somehow became combined with a trade fair during which the *toros bravos* were run through the street to the arena, and the most daring of the young men began to flirt with death along the way by seeing how close they could let the horns come to their bodies. The tradition persisted for centuries, a very Spanish anomaly known to few tourists. Then Gertrude Stein in Paris told Hemingway about the Fiesta of San Fermín; he went to it in 1924, and was enchanted. To his friend William Horne, Jr., he wrote:

We [are] the only foreigners at the damn fair. Every morning the bulls that are going to fight that afternoon are released from the corrals on the far side of town and race through the long main street of the town to the bull ring with all of the young bucks of Pamplona running ahead of them! A mile and a half run—all the side streets barred off with big wooden gates and all this gang going like hell with the bulls trying to get them.

By God they have bull fights in that town. There were 8 of the best toreros in Spain and 5 of them got gored! The bulls bagged just one a day.

You'd be crazy about a really good bullfight, Bill. It isn't just brutal like they always told us. It's a great tragedy—and the most beautiful thing I've ever seen and takes more guts and skill and guts again than anything possibly could. It's just like having a ringside seat at the war with nothing going to happen to you. I've seen 20 of them. Hash [Hadley] saw 5 at Pamplona and was wild about it.

He could hardly wait to get back the following year and wrote to another friend:

The godamdest wild time and fun you ever saw. Everybody in the town lit for a week, bulls racing loose through the streets every morning, dancing and fireworks all night and this last July us guys practically the guests of the city ... Honest to gawd Carper, there never is anything like it anywhere in the world. Bullfighting is the best damn stuff in the world.

Out of this enthusiasm came the novel *The Sun Also Rises*, published in 1926, which was a great success and put both Hemingway and Pamplona on the literary and touristic map forever. Because of the book and its romantic setting, thousands of Europeans and Americans made the July trip to Pamplona, two hundred miles from Madrid, and in 1988 it was estimated that some one hundred thousand tourists poured into this town. In 1944, when this writer first went to the Fiesta of San Fermín, there were no non-Spaniards running in front of the bulls. In 1988, a third of the runners were foreigners, and, unbelievably, some were women.

Since record-keeping began in 1591, fifty-two runners have been gored to death. There are no statistics for those almost killed, maimed or crippled.

Just a few miles from Pamplona is the charming village of Burguete where, in *The Sun Also Rises*, the characters Jake Barnes and Bill Gorton fished before joining their friends for the fiesta. Burguete, which has changed very little over the centuries, was a favorite of Hemingway's. He liked to recall swimming in the Irati near Aoiz, the "water clear as light," and the picnic in the beech forest where the ancient trees were "like drawings in a child's fairy book."

T*he fiesta was really started. It kept up day and night for seven days. The dancing kept up, the drinking kept up, the noise went on.*

—The Sun Also Rises

The godamdest
wild time and
fun you ever
saw. Everybody in the
town lit for a week, bulls
racing through the
streets every morning,
dancing and fireworks
all night . . .

— A letter from
Hemingway to a
friend in 1924

*I*t was the best party almost I've ever been on. Spaniards are the only people.

—Hemingway, in a
letter to Gertrude
Stein, July, 1925

Pamplona is no place to bring your wife. The odds are all in favor of her getting ill, hurt or wounded or at least jostled and wine squirted over her, or of losing her; maybe all three. If anybody could do Pamplona successfully it would be Carmen and Antonio but Antonio would not bring her. It's a man's fiesta and women at it make trouble, never intentionally of course, but they nearly always make or have trouble."

— Death in the
Afternoon

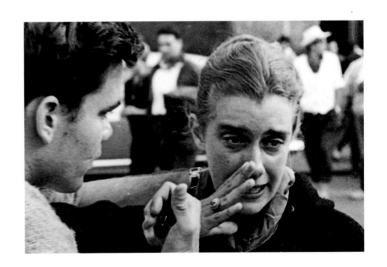

There are festivals and carnivals and holy days celebrating something or other in every country, but there are only two instances I know of when the name of the place and of the occasion are one and the same: Mecca and Pamplona.

Only Moslems are allowed in Mecca. You can get killed in Mecca if you aren't a Moslem. Anybody can make the pilgrimage to Pamplona and anybody can get killed. Anybody who runs with the bulls. No more comparisons are in order. Moslems don't drink—or aren't supposed to. In Pamplona, you drink and drink for seven days and seven nights, beginning noon July 6th when the first rocket goes up. You drink and you dance and you march in the procession behind St. Fermín—and you run with the bulls.

The bull-fight itself has a religious origin. Its ancestor is the Minotaur. The bullfighter is something of a priest. The Corrida is not to be regarded as a sport. Running with the bulls, however, is pure sport. You handicap yourself. the older, slower, less agile you are, the more distance you put between yourself and the bulls. The swifter, the nimbler you are, the later you start. One should not allow vanity to play an important role in this matter. Sixteen hundred weight of bone and muscle behind forty inches of horn with pin-sharp points can be very painful going up the arse and that's exactly what you're asking for when you choose to run ahead of twenty such monsters down a narrow street without egress!

Anywhere but Pamplona they'd call out the militia. But this is all-fools with drink-dance-caper-run with the bulls, spend your money, live it up, every man's your brother, every woman is your sister or your wife. No one shall go hungry or thirsty. Sleep briefly on your elbow.

—John Huston, in a
letter to Loomis
Dean, 1970

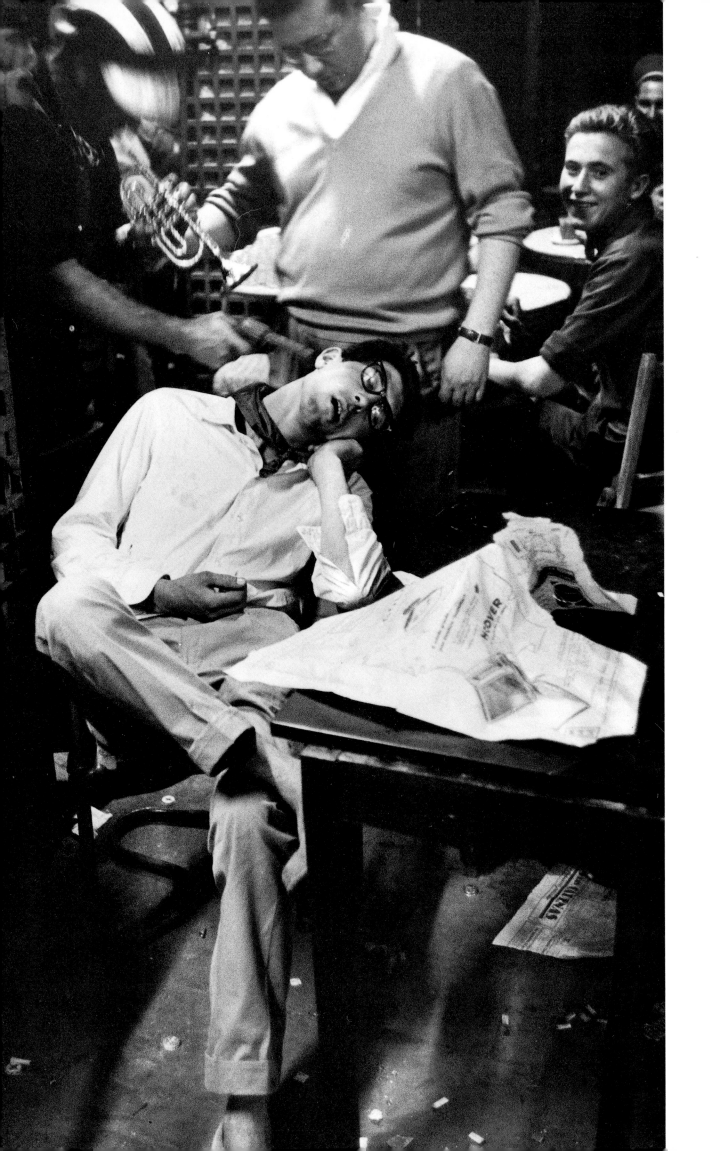

6:30 AM

*In an enthusiastic letter
to old friend and fellow
World War I ambulance
driver William Horne,
Jr., Hemingway wrote:
... have just got back
from the best week I
ever had since the
Section—the big Feria
at Pamplona—5 days of
bull fighting dancing all
day and all night—
wonderful music—
drums, reed pipes,
fifes—faces of
Velásquez's drinkers,
Goya and Greco faces,
all the men in blue shirts
and red handkerchiefs.*

Everyone has been
up all night and
now they are
refueling their
courage for the
run.

All the same, the Spaniards never lack the courage to make the heroic gesture. The bull is admired, almost worshipped, as the horse is in Ireland. He is admired because he is great and capable of fury, and the Spaniard requires that furious force against which to display his singularity—the most precious of his possessions—and his courage. Always an extremist, he likes to test his courage and his whole personality to the utmost, and he has so contrived the phases of the bullfight that each one has the crisis of decorative perfection that he loves.

— V. S. Pritchett, in
*The Spanish
Temper*

The run which will last
approximately six minutes
has begun.

7:00 AM

*Suddenly a crowd came
down the street. They
were all running,
packed close together . . .*

—The Sun Also
Rises

7:01 AM

Then they came in sight. Eight bulls galloping along, full tilt, heavy set, black, glistening, sinister, their horns bare, tossing their heads. And running with them three steers with bells on their necks.

—Hemingway, in
*The Toronto Star
Weekly*, 1923

7:03 AM

Then the bull will turn like a cat and get somebody who has been acting very brave about ten feet behind him. Then he will toss a man over the fence. Then he picks out one man and follows him in a wild twisting charge through the entire crowd until he bags him.

—Hemingway, in
The Toronto Star Weekly, 1923

7:05 AM

They ran in a solid mass, and ahead of them sprinted, tore, ran and bolted the rear guard of the men and boys of Pamplona who had allowed themselves to be chased through the streets for a morning's pleasure.

—Hemingway, in *The Toronto Star Weekly*, 1923

No one is
armed. No one
hurts or
plagues the bull in any
way. A man who
grabbed the bull by the
tail and tried to hang on
was hissed and booed by
the crowd and the next
time he tried it was
knocked down by
another man in the bull
ring. No one enjoys it all
more than the bull.

— Hemingway, in
*The Toronto Star
Weekly*, 1923

DEATH IN THE

AFTERNOON

our of his books, his only play, and some of his best stories take place in Spain, and in the foreground of that Spanish landscape is the atavistic art of *toreo*. Hemingway's attraction to that primordial spectacle was not a question, as Anthony Burgess fecklessly put it, of his "making the *corrida* exteriorize certain movements of his own soul." In fact, precisely the opposite was the case. The *corrida* set forth a pattern of experience, an archetype of experience, which recreated the oldest and most timeless myths which mankind had recorded. Gilgamesh who slayed the Bull of Heaven, Mithra who slayed the sacred white bull, Hercules who slayed the mad Cretan bull, Theseus who slayed the great bull of Marathon and then the Minotaur — these are but the tip of the iceberg of the myriad myths about and beliefs in the hero's sacrifice of the bull which in the Romantic theatre of the *plaza de toros* becomes, however, subliminally apparent to the *público*, reincarnate. Hemingway's visceral, immediate and intuitive response to that spectacle, his perfect description of the ecstasy of a great *faena*, his insistence on the feeling of life and death that the *corrida* gave him, and his inclusion of *toreo* as part of his inner life, indicate overwhelmingly that Hemingway's conception of *toreo* was, as were all the things that were most important to him, a spiritual matter, one of the "true" phenomena he discovered in a lifelong quest for eschatological certainty.

—Allen Josephs, in
*Hemingway
Review*, 1988

The bullfight audience is the most fickle in the world but also the most knowledgeable. They cannot be conned as they really do know all the aspects of "La Fiesta Brava." They can tell instantly when a bull storms into the ring if he is good or bad, if he hooks to the left or to the right, if he is brave or a coward (Ferdinand), if he is going to jump the fence, try to get out and not fight, they know and voice their disapproval. And this only applies to the bull and is not a patch to the abuse they lay on to the matador if he is shabby in his work.

—The Dangerous
Summer

All bullfighters begin in the lower depths, in the capeas in the little villages of Spain. They drift from capea to capea, carrying their clothes in a sack. They face tricky cows, fast and mean, and are judged by hard peasants who have paid for the bull and demand more than just entertainment. These capeas are the great trials for the aspiring bullfighters.

He killed badly and the crowd erupted and showered the plaza with pillows: a serious offence but obviously impossible to enforce. The fight had been a total disaster!

— The Dangerous Summer

The dictator's daughter and
the celebrated actress—
ardent fans of El Cordobés

I am sad and sorry that man for his soul's safety must test himself, his control and courage against this most ferocious and clever of all beasts but I am filled with a kind of elation, not that he must, but that he can and does. In so doing he grafts a little greatness on his audience.

— John Steinbeck, in "An Essay on Bullfighting"

The three matadors and their *cuadrillas* salute the president of the arena.

Behind the four horsemen came the procession of the bull fighters. They had been all formed in ranks in the entrance way ready to march out, and as the music started they came. In the front rank walked the three espadas or toreros, who would have charge of the killing of the six bulls of the afternoon.

They came walking out in heavily brocaded yellow and black costumes, the familiar 'toreador' suit, heavy with gold embroidery, cape, jacket, shirt and collar, knee breeches, pink stockings, and low pumps. Always at bull fights afterwards the incongruity of those pink stockings used to strike me. Just behind the three principals—and after your first bullfight you do not look at their costumes but their faces—marched the teams or cuadrillas. They are dressed in the same way but not as gorgeously as the matadors.

—Hemingway, in
The Toronto Star Weekly, 1923

Inside they all stood around in the bull ring, talking and looking up in the grandstand at the girls in the boxes. Some of the men had field glasses in order to look better.

—The Dangerous Summer

*T*he bullfight is not a sport in the Anglo-Saxon sense of the word, that is, it is not an equal contest or an attempt at an equal contest between a man and a bull. Rather it is a tragedy; the death of the bull, which is played, more or less well, by the bull and the man involved and in which there is danger for the man but certain death for the animal. This danger to the man can be increased by the bullfighter at will in the measure in which he works close to the bull's horns. . . . [the] danger of goring, which the man creates voluntarily, can be changed to certainty of being caught and tossed by the bull if the man, through ignorance, slowness, torpidness, blind folly or momentary grogginess breaks any of [the] fundamental rules for the execution of the different suertes.

—Death in the Afternoon

The bullfight is very moral to
me because I feel very fine
while it is going on and have
a feeling of life and death and mortal-
ity and immortality, and after it is
over I feel very sad but very fine.

— Death in the
Afternoon

The son of Hemingway's
Pedro Romero executes a
perfect *pass en redondo.*

A deadly dangerous performance only made possible by perfect nerves, judgement, courage and art.

—The Dangerous Summer

I could see he had the three requisites for a matador: courage, skill in his profession and grace in the presence of the danger of death.

—The Dangerous Summer

He had done it too many times in his imagination. Too many times he had seen the horns, seen the bull's wet muzzle, the ear twitching, then the head go down and the charge, the hoofs thudding and the hot bull pass him as he swung the cape, to recharge as he swung the cape again, then again, and again, and again, to end winding the bull around him in his great media-veronica, and walk swingingly away, with bull hairs caught in the gold ornaments of his jacket from the close passes . . .

— Hemingway, *The Capital of the World*

El Cordobés loses sight of the lethal horns for a moment as he executes a *chicuelina*.

It is impossible to believe the emotional, spiritual intensity and pure, classic beauty that can

...be produced by a man, an animal and a piece of scarlet serge draped over a stick. — Death in the Afternoon

El Cordobés, shown here, was not naturally graceful, but he valued and developed grace under pressure. And he was *under pressure, the enormous pressure of being* el número uno *every afternoon that he fought—and he fought almost every afternoon for over ten years.*

Bull fighting is an exceedingly dangerous occupation. In sixteen fights I saw there were only two in which there was no one badly hurt. On the other hand it is very remunerative. A popular espada gets $5,000 for his afternoon's work. An unpopular espada though may not get $500. Both run the same risks. It is a good deal like Grand Opera for the really great matadors except they run the chance of being killed every time they cannot hit high C.

— Hemingway, in
*The Toronto Star
Weekly*, 1923

H emingway is far more interested in the man, the matador, than in the bulls, in how the matador gets in trouble with the bulls and above all in how he dies on the horns of the bull. *For all its virtues and its splendid writing,* **Death in the Afternoon** *is foremost a fascinating necrology. Hemingway ransacked the ambiente for tales of blood, guts and death; the professional torero's view that a cornada may be heroic, but is more likely the result of stupidity is never broached in Hemingway's writing. That view probably would not have interested him, for his center of attention was elsewhere: not on toreo roundly and fully but on those aspects of toreo, men's behavior as he interpreted it, under stress.*

— John McCormick,
in *The Complete
Aficionado*

El Cordobés is carried
unconscious from the
Pamplona arena.

The great Cordoban's (Manolete's) death was a very Hemingwayesque one, and it reminded people once again that while seemingly one-sided and easy when performed by a master, bullfighting is still the most dangerous game in the world. In spite of penicillin and modern medical techniques, aspirant bullfighters are killed each year. And top matadors such as Carnicerito, José Mata, José Falcón, Morenito de Valencia, Paquirri, El Yiyo, and Pepe Cáceres have died in the ring since Manolete's death. And to refute those who say that the modern bull is inoffensive, on October 4, 1975 a two-year-old calf killed one of the truly great Spanish toreros, Antonio Bienvenida, in the little arena on a ranch near Madrid.

"It was here—right here on August 28, 1947, where the bull Islero and Manolete killed each other! He died killing and he killed dying."
—Custodian of the Linares arena

*B*ullfighting brings the exaltation great music does and great poetry. One carries for a time afterwards the satisfaction and the knowledge that man is no weakling in a dreadful world—that by his bravery, his versatility and his merits he has and can survive anything the world can bring against him.

— John Steinbeck, in "An Essay on Bullfighting"

A highlight for Hemingway was in Zaragoza when Ostos, one of the most popular *toreros* in Spain, dedicated a bull to him. A. E. Hotchner, who was traveling with Hemingway and gathering material for his book **Papa Hemingway,** *wrote:*

"On the day that Ostos brindied a bull to Ernest, Ernest rose in response to Ostos' outstretched hat and the bull ring gave him a spontaneous standing ovation, roaring his name; it was an awesome and moving sight to see those thousands of Spanish people, who do not express approval easily, on their feet, applauding an American. I think there were two reasons for this reaction: Ernest, as a non-Spaniard, had written about bullfighting, in **Death in the Afternoon,** *as well as any Spaniard ever had; and* **For Whom the Bell Tolls,** *banned by Generalissimo Franco and never published in Spain, so eloquently bespoke deep feelings long suppressed."*

154

The biographer Andre Turnbull wrote of Hemingway at this period of his life: "A great dignity flowed from his tall lurching frame and his sad mask of a face."

Yet here he is in Spain, in front of a bullfight poster, and he appears happy and vigorous and optimistic, though he is only a few months away from his death.

Back in Ketchum, Idaho, on July 2, 1961, the burden of being Ernest Miller Hemingway was finally more than he could bear, and he did away with the brain that was torturing him.

A visitor to his house today can see graphic proof of his love for Spain: a bullfight poster like the one in the background of this photo, two cocktail tables made of ancient taurine tiles, a bullfight painting by his friend Waldo Pierce, and countless framed photos of his matador friends and himself in Spain.

It is the house of a true Hispanophile—perhaps the truest of them all.

To me heaven would be a big bull ring with me holding two barrera seats and a trout stream outside that no one else was allowed to fish in and two lovely houses in the town; one where I would have my wife and children and be monogamous and love them truly and well and the other where I would have my nine beautiful mistresses on 9 different floors.

— Hemingway, in a
1925 letter to
F. Scott Fitzgerald